Eunice Andrada | Flood Damages

MW00657635

New Poems

GIRAMONDO POETS

Eunice Andrada | **Flood Damages**

First published 2018
from the Writing & Society Research Centre
at Western Sydney University
by the Giramondo Publishing Company
PO Box 752 Artarmon NSW 1570 Australia
www.giramondopublishing.com

© Eunice Andrada 2018

Designed by Harry Williamson
Typeset by Andrew Davies
in 10/16.5 pt Baskerville BT

Printed and bound by Ligare
Distributed in Australia by NewSouth Books

Cataloguing-in-Publication data is available
from the National Library of Australia

ISBN 978-1-925336-66-5

Cover art by Marikit Santiago
Photographer Cassie Bedford

All rights reserved.
No part of this publication may be
reproduced, stored in a retrieval system
or transmitted in any form or by any means
electronic, mechanical, photocopying or
otherwise without the prior permission of
the publisher.

For my mothers, Dinna and Chona

Contents

flood damages

a series of half-truths about drowning

saltwater will lick your wounds willingly

Can I tell you I loved him because he looked familiar?
This ocean paid no mind to the bloodline I wore
around my neck. Only eager for the salt of me.
He made a tourniquet from his body.
Swathed it around mine.
He siphoned his spit into my pores.
I floated a while.

you will know when they begin to struggle breathing

Morning has barely dragged its limbs through the
curtain and Angelina is sitting up on her straw mat.
She raises her milky irises past the ceiling and to
her god. Her throat, a busted faucet, the worship
dribbling from her lips. The floor is wet with hymns.
Every morning she is a vessel emptied. Angelina rises
from the linoleum, rolls up her bed and waits for
breakfast. It is another day in another woman's house.
She gathers her limbs into walk, then into ritual.
No one can decipher the shapes she makes from her

mouth. Her niece pays for her meal that night.
When they find her lying cold on the mat one morning,
the god is gone from her lips.
Blessed be the faithful who flood their ancient lungs
with prayer
then swim to the nearest voice.

those who live by the water die by the water

I am tired of the part of the song where I am made
the water where gentiles wash their feet.
I stand in the ocean and cradle
the loss of us. Here is the gash that tears wider
as you tell its story. The people drink in the water burial
then rise, light as before.

for my womb

An offering spilled
into navy blue film
my age, date of visit
the exact diameter
of coiled tissue *inside*

I am sixteen
when my body remembers *it is October*
the mothers it belongs to
they say the diagnosis stained
our blood memory
skirting beneath scorched irises *and you*
you saw the bleeding from afar
and breathed it horizon

To be woman is to be studied
and proven wrong. *Matris*, you *are a full moon*
remind me I am capable of inheritance
I wish you ghost
I wish you chamomile and grain
I want to show these photographs
to my somewhere-daughter
watch her grin
pool like candle wax
on your ruined bed

a room for each prayer

It must have been after the sermon
wrung us dry
his lungs an emptying congregation
as I mouthed sins into my fingers
and waited
for the syrup of three
Our Fathers, two Glory Bes
to settle on the ground

/

They don't do with stained glass around here
around here the bent knee is its own altar
and I am made walking stick nightly
doing with the recitations
if catatonia *ask for another towel*
if varicose veined *praise the earthworms*
if thirsty *rehearse Maya's second memoir*
if barren *ask for another consequence*
to your skin

/

It must have been after the sermon
wrung us dry

that I remembered we slept here
the evidence of cicada shells under pillows
leftover harmonies on my cheek
I spend a thank you

/

I know there is no balcony
from which to taste the dingy fruit of smoke
you let me in anyway
and there is the collision of nape and wood
children have softer bones, she chides

but it can't be true
I am tender
and unmiraculous but whole
I say none of this and listen to the class laugh
their instinct for hysteria
when they see the bird-boned
choke on flight

/

when he opens his mouth
to renounce my god
I ask to continue the conversation

in bed, where I close my eyes
and fool my bones into worship

/

the body, a sacred mass
strung and latticed by sundried prayer
afloat in a roomful of cavities
jars of oil on the ground
paused until the question of the fig
is felt behind teeth

(because I am a daughter) of diaspora

and by default –
an open sea,
what language will not meet me
with rust?

They convince my mother
her voice is a selfish tide,
claiming words that are not meant
for her,

this roiling carcass of ocean
making ragdolls of our foreign
limbs.

In the end
our brown skin
married to seabed.

When I return to the storm
of my islands
with a belly full of first world,
I wrangle the language I grew up with
yet still have to rehearse.
I play with the familiar rattle of consonants

on my tongue and do not think myself
a serpent.

By the street corner, a man in rags
speaks to me in practised English.
Where are you going?

I don't respond,
the words a recognition
of the mongrel flag
I call my face.
I want to say to him, *We are the same.*
Pareho lang po tayo.
My bleached accent,
the dollars in my wallet
sing another anthem.

How long have you been here?

How long are you staying?

I am above water, holding
onto a country that drowns
with or without me.

first creation

in my sister's hand-me-down pyjamas
morning wrapped
in worn-out cotton
breakfast before school

my brother the prophet
sits unspeaking beside me
daydreams of Israel
or some other violent video game

Ma sits across from us
my father stands behind her, his hand
on the back of her chair

they talk about the news
Ma says the word 'tsunami'
her mongrel tongue
birthing the word
in a new body

my father corrects her
it's an alien climate
a year & a half here

when the bottom of the pan
cracks against my mother's head
I forget what she said just before

something about the news
the steel pan connects to my father's hand
no one says a word

no television drone to muffle her shame
the prophet eats beside me
I am too small for my age
Ma always says I should eat more

she doesn't look at us
we are ten minutes away from school
if we walk

novena for her sickness

O anesthesia, I am in love
with the way muscle caves
to the whim of scalpel.
You must hear me
in my vilest seasons.
Send my love to the chemicals
you breed from my fragile.
Please bring them to say hello.

O lupus, don't look at me
like you looked at her –
one of my mother's multitude
of mothers – as though
I, too, were a constellation
of open wounds.

There is a room, swarmed
in antiseptic light.
Then, a family split
shucked when the light leaves.

O lupus, I can't recall the colour
her walls were painted.
May you let me remember this,
at least, and you can forget
where I live.

habeas corpus

you will see me   & say   I haven't changed
your hair longer   than mine   I will tell you
I got sensitive skin   you insist   it's okay then teach me
your beauty   routines   prosecco shimmer on top
of my cheekbones   amberglow   on the centre of my eyelids

in a few minutes   I break out   in ultra-strobed hives
rashes populating   the apples of my cheeks   glitter snagged in sun
your apology   silent   it's my skin that reacted first
to borrowed makeup   we will choose   not to talk

about the day your clothes   stopped reeking   of the operating bed
how the doctor woke you,   *you may have   the body*
you may   have   your body

I will be in your sweater   when I tell you   I'm a virgin
you will say   quieter   your brother's drunk friend
took you at a party &   you didn't know   what to do so you let him

& show me   the riot of scar   tissue under your belly the
darling   carved into your jaw   we come from women
who didn't   choose   their bodies

sister we leave   no songs   behind
we   remember   ourselves
every   unfurling   anatomy

last days of rain

stormwater-blessed children
baptised in ruptured sky
ripped from the throat of a typhoon
before it could swallow them

and what of those left behind
la niña
cathedral
bullethole

the womb is a gutted church
for a choir of lonesome children
their god, a foul-mouthed father

if you tell your children
the story of how you came here
in a language they don't understand
did you arrive at all?

here are the displaced:
feet bruised with the rhythm of leaving
skin dusted with pacific salt
from islands that call back
in a different voice

this country moves its children's lips
with nursery rhymes of whiteness
which is to say
forgetfulness is an easy meal

you ravenous prayer
you secondhand anthem
passed into a prodigal tongue

do you remember the smell of sampaguitas
sold from grime-covered knuckles?
how they remind you of Sunday afternoons
a reprieve from the smoke?

how familiar it was to mute the smell of burning
with flowers
how silent it is when we begin to forget
thirsting for oceans that will not know
our names

honeysuckle

It is the kind of awake
that dives into us
not wanting to surface for air.
Searchlight fingers burn want
into my breath;
he tells me I am rare
like I was made to be found.

My body is a colosseum
breaking into applause
when the beasts draw blood;
the blood comes with an audience
of thieves. They have screamed for me
to cast off my flesh in shame.

I've rebuilt your cathedrals
re-written your hymns
left nothing but my name to sing.
Here, my blood is the wine
I drink my love creation
I drink my love resurrection
I drink my love the eighth day
when life pulsed reckless
after becoming.

His mouth teasing the climax
from my body
I am my own
deity in the dark
not waiting for an ending.

When my naked is coiled into his naked
and he is soaked in me
I tell him my blood is no coincidence.

alibi

When he says he doesn't want me, I gather
the plants on our balcony.
Offer my blood as an easy alibi
for the broken door, the vase, the picture frames,
my wrists.
Blame the muscle memory of dancing
to the gospel
of my father's temper.
I wash my hair
in vinegar.

etymology

family gatherings
chock-full of abbreviation

titas / titos
indays / manongs

names spliced &
multiplied / rearranged

Ting Ting / Nonoy
Toto / Ging Ging

Ma names us after
those in the Old Testament

renames us over the sinigang
and bagoong

biblical code
made digestible

birth names wriggling
in between floorboards

like tails of a *butiki*
thrice

my grandmother knocks
on the wall

second coming

I am off the coast of an island eight hours from my grandmother's old Parañaque apartment. The boatman says I swim well and beckons me to go underwater. He wants me to see what he sees. I unclip my vest and dive. Here, the world is prismatic and unspeaking. I kick my legs into a school of fish. It erupts into blue confetti before drawing together again. There are corals that look like bullions of gold; I remind myself, they, too, are homes for smaller creatures. There is the unrelenting deep and the uncertainty of return. There is my half-brother, Lemuel. Another love the ocean refused to return. I break the water's skin and reintroduce myself to air. I thank him for guiding me. We make the quiet journey back to the mainland, where I plan to waste my money on cheap cocktails and souvenirs. My friend sings under her breath, just loud enough to hear over the motor engine. It is late afternoon and there is the ocean, surrounding us like a reminder. The boat slows to a halt metres from the shore. The boatmen draw the ladder down to the water and begin to thank us, ushering light-skinned hands down the vessel. One of them turns to me, asks where my mother is from. *Iloilo*. He nudges the other boatman and they smile, say they could tell from the way I speak. I am reminded of my mother's hurt.

How it never failed to sound like a river, no matter how broken her voice had become. How the name for the people she had come from translates to *where the water flows down*. The boatman says he can tell from the way I speak. I look to my feet. They are lost underwater.

preparations

you see how pressed flower he has become
after the fourth year of his disappearance
this is asphyxia / to choke on the welcome mat of your throat
he pulls you close as an afterthought

after the fourth year of his disappearance
you wait for your half-brother's body to surface in an email
he pulls you close as an afterthought
remember how the water scalded your brother, but never you?

you will wait for his body to surface in an email
he taught you to lust only for his forgiveness
remember how the ocean was doused in him, not you?
there are colours named after the work of his hands

he taught you to lust only for his forgiveness
you let him laugh at your interrogations
there are colours named after the work of his hands
you notice how pressed flower he has become

soft departure

the first and last

time immigration

knocks on our door

ma confesses

there were three

of them

one of her

five of us

earlier that day

she mashes chicken liver

into sliced bread

picks us up from school

commits no crimes

she volunteers to

leave

they thank her

before they go

ma wishes

she had trained

as a singer

tells me to croon

into empty

spaces

wait for her return

pilgrim sweat

autopsy

Ma loads her gun with aratelis berries
shoots at Noy till the wildfruit explode
against his hair, then keeps shooting.
Syrup and rind spray against
their too-small shirts,
curl into the webs of their toes.

It is just after siesta and their backs
have been clapped with talcum powder.
The air is overripe
everything bruised and liable
to burst at the slightest touch.
Point of sale.

When dark begins to pour
around their laughter,
they abandon the wreaths of mosquitoes
that call them holy.
Splotches of juice blacken the soil,
punctuating the walk
to the dinner table.
In that festering summer, Ma learns
the futility of sweetness.

Ma is at work in another continent
when a dictator is buried in the Heroes
Cemetery.
State-sanctioned killings begin
in her hometown. Twenty-six shots
to the head, chest, thighs
of two men.

I complain about the weather here,
how the cold leaves my knuckles parched.
Ma points to the fruit she bought over
the weekend, tells me I must eat.

bedtime stories for my stretchmarks

In the beginning
there was the argument
between hard and soft

the young animal of your bones
yawning open
unfurling towards the sunlight

in between. You will learn
there is no safety
when you are something to be claimed.

You expect to be caught in the aftermath
of a crash
instead there is just

the echo of fault lines
rippling still
indelible marks of eruption.

You see how you wear rapture
all lovely and whole
as though it wasn't born

from the same war that made you.
How the hard and soft of you
were paralysed in embrace

to hold you still.
Yours are the hands of pilgrims
on the mornings you trust the freedom

of your skin, enough to come back to it.
You find yourself returning
to where the gentle left garlands

on your thighs as thanks
to the corners where your bones whispered
become.

Forgive your universe;
how it must collapse into your body
to find praise.

poem in which I,

the living narrator, occur in the context of still-here,
in the context of insufficient evidence, in the context
of not enough of him found on her lips, in the context
of splayed open, obvious, like that for a reason, in
the context of twelve Hail Marys dripping down your
navel, in the context of moonlight washed sober, in
the context of exhausted light in the 24/7 carnival
where you are the main attraction. You, girl, in the
context of dosage control, daffodil in and of itself, his
non-apology clotting up in your teeth, in the context
of no quiet ending, in the context of *can't you see I'm*
trying to save me for later, in the context of black hair,
brown girl, unfair and lovely, in the context of the day
you will be forgotten; you forget the *beautiful* another
boy says after he pulls away, his eyes closed for longer.
What won't he see – in the context of sunspots, stretch
marks, the continents smeared ugly on your back;
Mongolia, the knife, the right gene succession. You
are one in ten thousand martyrs, eggshell hollow and
dripping in exchange for meat, bent in the ways they
imagined you disrupted, in the context of the tightest
clothes you can borrow, you the historian, in the
context of stolen paper napkins, crammed between
your thighs. How much longer will this sound like
truth? You ask the book and it asks for your spine, says

ask elsewhere, seek the map detailing the false tragedy – stillbirth – still you call yourself a survivor, narrating in the context of ache, *or*, tomorrow.

harbour

Later, the doctor says to Ma
she fractured her arm years ago
without her knowing.
The points of impact sprawl
across the report:

Over the Banzai cliffs of Saipan,
five children and their kites
ensnared in the wind,
hair woven into milkteeth.

Below, soldiers who dove
into a cutting-board sea.
Sons turned shoreline in a crack.
Long gone before flight.

Ma is back in the car, stretching
clothes over broken capillaries.
Pasa sounds like the word
for *soaked*.
Ma's skin is soaked
in potholes.
She hears the ocean through the windows.

Later, two children by the water
in Puerto Azul. Blue Harbour.

We are distracted by the jellyfish
flooding the sand.
We hurl their pale corpses into our targets
dead bodies morphing into ammunition

mid-air and missing.
We wash our hands before dinner-table
grace.

Ma is back in the car, making
sure any material is stretched over
her shadowed limbs.
When he says he is sorry
before telling me to come inside,
his words lay stillborn in my palms.
They know how to play
with dead things.

forms

It is no sacrifice
when he collapses over his own altar
then asks for your body.

alternate texts on my aunt's lightening cream

top ten white sand tourist beaches
coloniser's ejaculate
pretty enough to be a halfie
where is your dad from
genocide the white lie
asian white lady horror trope
sexy singles near you
two-for-one exfoliating body scrub
fetish search term
papaya benefits on skin
calamansi benefits on skin
glutathione billboards
mestiza money
telenovela contrabida
genetic lottery win
first-class slave
the right kind of asian
gagged on a white flag

iha you look negro
bones the colour red
egg wash on pastry sheets
are you sure you're my daughter
drink some water scrub your face
icarus skin
o oceania your body an apartment block
cracked under the spanish the british the
americans the japanese the americans
all you do is fuck breed and beg
your reflection in the typhoon water
no water when you are burning
cast as maid yaya street gossip
spawn of the isaw vendor
clickbait jailbait
fetish search term
selling coal by the bag before school
who do you belong to

novena for fidelity

After we make love
when he traces the borders
of my architecture

without sight,

let it not be to seek
the fire escapes in me.
My god, must I lose

myself in this chalice?

When he begins to spill himself
onto my shaking,
he feels closest

to past tense.

I am not asked
to wash myself clean after.
He has already baptised me

in her image.

The kerosene she leaves,
my own dead sea to walk.

We are done with the acts of temptation.

All three end with burned sugar.

I rise and cough out her name
in the morning.
Forgive me

if this is more of a ritual

than my asking of penance.
My God, let me be more
than a blazing sacrifice

to his god.

How she must wait in the crevices
of our bedroom
and taunt her way into our silence.

Is there a love that will not leave me

lonely?
Let him find warmth
by these cinders

else burn with me.

photo album

Ferdinand Marcos crouches
retrieving
golf club for unknown woman, Navy Golf
Club, 1986

girl sticks origami insects
to third temporary address in
six months singing
Nina, 2016

woman cuts her hair
on balcony, Abu Dhabi, 2009

earthworms recoil over head free
fall forge crescent-shaped rashes
on subject's cheeks (seen above), August

dusty-eyed
woman shells hard-boiled egg in
empty room, Singapore, 2001

girl in bathroom sheds baby

pink lingerie reveals

allergic reaction across ribs, 1998

mother in robe writes email home

imagining herself in Spain listening

to castanets click

moths

outside slam their bodies

against glass door, 2012

woman (right) watches

her lover (left)

paint a foreign sky,

unknown location

author (right)

confuses her irises for vases

pokes stems

into mud of her

pupils, March

an exquisite corpse in which I disappear after each line

the fifteenth month, there are maggots
on the ceiling
you say it's because of the weather
not because you didn't take out the trash
for weeks

in another drenched country it is August
redworms drag their bellies across the ceiling
then fall at will, right into our cracked pores
leaving pink bubbling masses
in their wake

they curl into themselves
when they hit the floor
like spiralled incense
protecting their undersides
with the shell on their back
before we end their writhing
beneath our shoes

the maggots stay in our house for weeks
some mornings we climb onto the kitchen counter
and fold them into paper towels
we pop their bodies with our fingers
dump them in the trash

we are in bed when you say it's over
I talk around it and we talk through it
again. The following night we make love
trying to relearn how to speak
over an empty banquet table
and I don't come
clean the same way

we twist ourselves from the thick
material of our cheeks
when you say *palagi*
I curl into myself
you don't notice the smoke

roots: a new taxonomy

To learn a new reflection, one must lose the memory of hair
its tendency to gnarl on the scalp
with what it is dealt. See, cum crowning
glory – there are softer things with which to burden your head
like tattered scarves.
Choose the unpicked cotton field.

Unlearn the translations
of your skin. *Boca*,
buka, all the same
it will be asked of you.
You won't understand why
their work on your spine earned
the praise it did
but you know your muse has that effect.

The search engine will tell you
this abuse is a fetish
candy
to the ones who can orgasm
to the sight of you choking.

If you were white it would be called a crime but you aren't
and music

has no colour, remember?
has no colour, remember?

Your grandmother's howl has its footnote,
mapping out the rupture from cavity
to cavity.

Memorialise
what you can.
You will be taught legacy
in the porn sub-category
your sister's abuse can crawl into.

Ratings will say you are no more   than black-blue orifice
and they cup their lips beneath you,
starving for the scandal
of your ~~cunt~~ complexion.

To learn a new reflection,
be vast as the ~~territories~~ mothers
they named for you.
When he gazes at your skin
and asks to taste you,
become a mirror
ask if he can swallow.

draft instructions for when I leave

originally performed with my grandmother's clothes
haloed around my feet

origami my limbs
into the closest shape to here
press your fingers down to forge new angles
only use your nails if you have to / then
turn me inside out

or

dream of rapture and what you can take
if I have left you poetry
empty my pockets of stones

walk into a nameless ocean
remember me differently
when the salt dries

or

look to where you have known
to find me: in the corner of a shared room
writing the light back into my body
I will have a cup of ginger tea for you
it will still be warm

know that you will trade my face
with your eyes closed and see
the lovers whose hair you stroked and stroked
until you lost them to sleep / then
love

imagine I am somewhere waiting
wearing your favourite expression:
eyebrows hiked up like a skirt
eyes reflecting smoke
like they were staring
at fireworks

or

remember I don't like dancing
in the same place twice
unless I am with you
unless it is under the crooning rain
and tired streetlights
find me elsewhere

or

nowhere at all
the blueprint lost in the places

you forget to touch
when we make love

or

leave everything
the way it was
if I say goodbye
it is only to hear me say it
I have always been here

to cut the apples into eighths
deliver them to chapped lips
in the afternoon

or

remember I have been with you
through every honest ending

ode to the dark cunt

You press your lips to the Black Sea
drink in the last hours of light
until dusk trails down your chin

what do you tell them as you spread
your slick mouth
trickle secrets into open throats?
you whimper in your sleep
as you dream of the end of the world

come summer
thighs chafe
a Black Sea leads to your womb

in colder times
you are shrouded in polyester then
denim, muffling the inhale
exhale from your mouth
you search inside me for oxygen

they propose a salve of milk
aloe vera, lemon
you close your lips

when I am alone
I marvel at how the lighter skin of my fingers
disappears into your wet earth
I call this *miracle*
I call this *cure*

Oh, dark cunt
I have run from the ones who flinched
at the sight of you
splayed and waiting
your lips heavy
with honeyed liquor
we have learned to love the ones who offer up
their necks without us asking

oh true north,
you teach me my hunger is no mistake
I follow it to a paradise burnished black gold
anointed with the eclipse
midas cunt
everything you swallow
is left hungry

Prescription

believe him when he hurts you
believe him when he hurts you
believe him when he hurts you
believe him when he hurts you
believe him when he hurts you
believe him when he hurts you
believe him when he hurts you
believe him when he hurts you
believe him when he hurts you
believe him when he hurts you
believe him when he hurts you
believe him when he hurts you
believe him when he hurts you
believe him when he hurts you
believe him when he hurts you
believe him when he hurts you
believe him when he hurts you
believe him when he hurts you
believe him when he hurts you
believe him when he hurts you
believe him when he hurts you
believe him when he hurts you
believe him when he hurts you
believe him when he hurts you
believe him when he hurts you

water births

where are you from?

a woman's ribs / cheating grandfathers /
the confession box / floodwater

Marcos conducts my allergy test

Drawing a blue pen down the insides of my wrists. The pressure like a trail of ant bites drilling into the dark teal of veinwork. It is my second visit this week. The nurse doesn't make eye contact, just goes on listing odd numbers into the crude boxes he makes. *Did you forget to clean it?* I look at the tube of alcohol wipes on the shelf behind him. He gets up to 23 and lifts the pen from the grid. There is some fussing around small cases of instruments. A series of motions around and away from my body, then a set of needles materialises in his hands. I watch his fingers as he pricks the tip into the centre of each square canvas on my forearm. Punches the metal just past the surface then swiftly replaces the needles with new ones after they poke holes into me. He doesn't answer. Retrieves a case of vials instead and sorts through them. His badge reads *Ferdinand*.

Maybe he grew up here and my accent isn't quite right yet, so he can't understand me. Of course. Ferdinand takes the vials one by one and drops a single clear liquid onto the punctures. I ask him about the meaning of the colours on each vial and he says the doctor will explain. When he finishes dropping samples of the allergens on me, the beads of liquid lay suspended in their makeshift cells. He tells me to wait, exiting the room to drink water out of a powdery plastic cup. Later my skin is a one-way window and from the inside, someone smears scorching oil on my wrists. Later the flamenco begins, a slew of cherry red skirts flaring up one by one. *Wait a little longer*, Ferdinand says, his mouth still half-inside the cup when he re-emerges. I decline his offer of water. *You can move if you want to*. He packs the vials back into the box and disappears from the room again, his jeans and sneakers floating away from my periphery. I keep my arms propped up on the pillow and see them simmer in the poison. The holes bear scarlet gifts – at times shallow wells of blood, other times the leftover pulp of bruised fruit, eaten anyway. How I want to scrape the red debris of skin into my nails. How satisfying it is to see my body lurch and swell, activated by my own touch.

When Ferdinand returns and touches me, it is to prove I have no control over my skin. He pushes the bottom of a pen across my arm and, within a few seconds, a pink line protrudes from where he traced. Ferdinand chuckles. He makes a note of something and hands me a paper. *Give this to your doctor.* I thank him and finally stand, stretching my battered limbs.

After a short wait a man mispronounces my name and I know to respond, following him into another room. The sterile light hits the back of my throat and stays there. The doctor reads the results I hand to him. This one has no name attached to his shirt. He looks at me through rice grain eyes that remind me of my grandfather's. I look closer at how his skin pleats over the bones of his face and see his resemblance to the nurse. *Where are you from?* I had yet to speak to him. I open my mouth – *Perhaps you should re-consider your stay here*. The doctor says I am allergic to something in the air. To the foreign dirt. To four types of grass. I tell him my mother was deported once before, has since come back and still gets allergies like mine. She only gets them here. He says the skin I wear isn't the skin I came with. His lips form the words mechanically, like he has said this before. I tell him the sun here has already caused my birthmarks to morph. Oil slicks on floodwater. *You'll continue to react this way if you remain here, unless you take medication daily.* The doctor asks me if I want to see a specialist. I say I will think about it. He writes me a referral anyway, hands brisk, eyes not rising to mine. My forearms throb as more red-eyed dew percolates from the puncture marks. This time the ants on my skin are real. They break off chunks of the crimson pulp and carry their food away in an unending line. The doctor says nothing. I leave. He watches in silence as my skin disappears into the lights.

the prophet forgets her name

says no, he doesn't see the point
of helping women turned overripe
under men's fists
says he knows no-one who has
gone through that
We are in the living room
He asks if I want tea
Because he can get me some too
His eyes not leaving the screen as he slaughters
intergalactic demons in Doom 3

Inflamed spots litter his cheeks
pus-filled and scarred
He is excused for his startling
youth

The prophet is forgetful
I ask him
He gives me few words

Another time I scream at the prophet
He says I act this way because I haven't been
hit yet
His hands wrapped around a controller
my hair

The prophet leaves
his mark on me –
busted lips
pierced scalps
nail marks on ankles
– and forgets

I am told it is the role of brothers
to serve divine punishment
Ma was told women are meant to serve
their husbands

He speaks of an end
I am not part of
The prophet erases me
from scripture

rearrangement

on number 4, the AC bellows
mothball-scented relief
settings 1 to 3 not working
in my sister's car
my ma drives under a foreign sun
I alternate between killing the AC
and rolling my windows down
or blasting my face with the cool odour

at the stoplight she rubs her fair, waxy arms
clicks her tongue, *too hat*
as soon as I get to her place she tells me
to drink a glass of water
she boils lentils and pours in
the coconut milk
then meat, if there are leftovers

she tells me to open the lights
in the dining room and I don't correct her
we chew on the curried grains
and mistranslate

she is patient when it takes me
a few moments to say things like *hinihingal*
I disfigure the words in my mouth

until I too deliver them in new bodies
when we speak, it is all accent and
rearrangement
she translates and reconsiders
and again
saturating one language with another

what careful, imperfect truths
we have birthed in this prose of error
and *say it again, please*

still she says *kwento ka pa, anak*
when I finish a story
and I do
the times I mangle her mother tongue
to her face, unflinching

portrait of Lilia as Mata Hari

Passing through the x-ray machine   a heap of her
finest flesh dropped to the black
plastic when she shudders
in an alien climate.

Mata Hari takes her shoes off
for no one. Uncorks the bullets
from her frontal lobe instead   giggles
champagne when they ask her to unclasp
the gold from her ears.
She peels off the layers of clothing
& they cast the sensor over her body.

Mata Hari leaves airport security
all metal   obsidian hair cut short.
A new man waits. Men believe
only in the dancer's body
not the apocalypse she bends to.
Mata Hari dances
like a parable repeated:
I am everything
you think I am.

Mata Hari sends x-ray scans
of her lungs to the Immigration Department

every three months. A gift of peacekeeping
from a fickle lady with joint pains.
I greet your silver
with my collars down,
my jugular for you to see.

Mata Hari bends to the earth
presses her sinewed hands
into the ground and feels the drumming,
the marionette clap of approval.
What else is there left to show?

Perhaps a new history
to wash down the hollow.
In an alternate ending, Mata Hari
was not a heartbroken lover
whose chest was made an orchard
of bullets.
Not a dancer, but a teacher
to children whose palms did not know
casualty.

On some days the favourite mestiza whore,
but the woman you trust
not to stain your wife's dress.

Mata Hari takes portraits of herself
every morning, tracing where
the fault lines begin.

Her English
trips over a stiff-necked accent.
Imagine every bone
is tethered to a star,
your machinery pulled taut
against the night sky.
This is how you keep your spine
straight.

After her third year as an unfamiliar,
no one has asked *how.*
She is asked why, so she gives them stale bread.
Asked who, so she turns the lights off.

Mata Hari remembers the rice-grain eyes
of her first child.
She cries when I dedicate this poem to her.
She does not understand the words.

Mata Hari calls me
when her husband has two strokes
in the middle of the night,
her voice crushed to red and blue.

She lay awake the night after,
her husband still on a hospital bed.
The doors to her home are bolted shut,
her promised land now
a den of thieves.

What becomes of the woman
who comes from the rib of man?
When Mata Hari refuses to speak
she is dashed to pieces
of pottery;
back to shattered clay.

Mata Hari is both the hand that feeds
and the hand-fed fable.
Mata Hari dances to music swollen
with a language she did not teeth on.

She is laced around the riffs like smoke
cradles the drumming between her thighs
dances apocalyptica
in a dusty living room.

There are no mirrors.

Just her body
gluttonous and beating,

dancing her queendom
to an empty court.

Mata Hari turns off the music,
listens for the weather next morning.
There is laundry to fold
in the next room.
The men are asleep.

I visit Mata Hari on Sunday afternoons.
She teaches me to pick blueberries from a tree branch
that hangs over her fence.
She brings the berries to her lips and closes
her eyes, waiting for the sweet.

for my womb (reprise)

this is the truth
of the body:
a weightless child finds
its way out of my skin
and there is no funeral

just the blood on my thighs that I make
a habit of wiping away
before it hits the bathroom floor

each child is named after the month
my skin sirens a repeat
of wadded tissue
of moonlit cleansing
the habit of miscarriage

he holds me between the stovetop
and last night's dirty dishes
there is no baby
spills from his lips on cue
as though the mourning could
not begin if only I
were in attendance

and to think because of a pill
I will only be a daughter to lose
more daughters

this is the season
my body is convinced I am with child
this is the season of leaving
when I hear the call of *mother*
escape a bruise full of mouths

novena for my mother's collarbones

Hear that I must
use another woman's anatomy
to examine my own hurt.

It is the surgery I swallow
to flay the wreckage, Lord
because we are made of You,
her blood is my blood
her flesh, my flesh.

O, the brutalities that have left us mosaic
the blame men have left to curdle
in our marrow.

Lord, here is my mother's right
collarbone
the part of her that didn't suffer
permanent trauma
from the time her husband
thundered his fists against her;
left her partially deaf.

Take this and remake me whole.
Let me be
in my own garden.

Womb of wombs,
I have run to your stained glass
and seen funhouse mirror.

Maker of hands that hurt us,
do you hear the chords in me struck
down when she can't breathe?

My God, I am trying to keep in tune
while singing around the broken glass
of gospel music.

Can you hear the amen in this
alone?

last meal before deportation

if there was a final dinner with my mother
before she left, I cannot recall it
but I can picture five brown bodies
and their light-skinned mother
embracing over the grimy carpet

I can't remember what we ate for dinner
but I know she would have scoured
the fridge for substitute ingredients
if I had asked for my favourite dish

I know my mother would have told us
to hold each other's hands
as she prayed in two languages

how my mother must have felt her mother's
rosemary beads grind against her throat
as she breathed
testing idle hopes in her accent
seetisen, *citizen*
mader, *mother*

choking back and eating the labels
dirty immigrant, illegal, TNT
so they would not find our plates

the night would have been the beginning
of our exodus
a generation of daughters
left behind

recognition

my grandmother teaches me how
to break dried marigolds open
and plant the seeds in shallow soil
her English sharpened against years
of mangled Frank Sinatra lyrics
and American blockbusters

her accent wraps needles
around the soft syllables
as she asks me to pick more
flowers for her

on trains she speaks to me
as though we were
in her living room in Parañaque
walls saturated with her volume
couches draped with sheets
para hindi mag-amoy tao
– so it doesn't smell like people
live here –

her language turns heads
in the carriage I wait
for someone to tell us
to go back to where we came from

I will only find my mouth
its own country snarled
in borders

Acknowledgements

For the single mothers, the undocumented immigrant parents, the survivors of trauma after trauma, flood after flood, and for the quiet brown girl with the stubborn accent, forever caught between cultures – this is for you.

Thank you to the editors of *Peril Magazine*, *Verity La*, *Mascara Literary Review* and *Red Room Poetry*, where early versions of these poems have appeared.

I would especially like to thank my mother for the countless sacrifices she has made for our family. Thank you for teaching me what it means to love – across oceans, despite distance and difference. My infinite thanks also goes to my grandmother for raising me with Taglish, for singing to me in Tagalog, for teaching me Ilonggo. Thank you to my three sisters, who stand tall among the strongest, most resilient women I know.

Thank you to my mentors and inspirers Candy Royalle, Tamryn Bennett, Merlinda Bobis, Ivy Alvarez, Michelle Cahill, Tanya Evanson, Eileen Chong, Lorin Reid and Kirli Saunders.

Thank you to my wonderful friends Kim Trang, Chris Wright, Wanyi Xin, Kristy Wan, Michelle Meng, Christine Villareal, Diane Macabugao, Johnrey Almonte, Gloria Demillo – this brown immigrant girl couldn't have made a home here without you.

My gratitude goes to Colin Ho, for the sublime opportunity to love you and be loved by you, in all of our shared and unshared languages.

The Giramondo Publishing Company acknowledges the support of Western Sydney University in the implementation of its book publishing program.

This project has been assisted by the Commonwealth Government through the Australia Council, its arts funding and advisory body.